Skyscrapers

by Chris Bowman

BELLWETHER MEDIA • MINNEAPOLIS, MN

Note to Librarians, Teachers, and Parents:

Blastoff! Readers are carefully developed by literacy experts and combine standards-based content with developmentally appropriate text.

Level 1 provides the most support through repetition of high-frequency words, light text, predictable sentence patterns, and strong visual support.

Level 2 offers early readers a bit more challenge through varied simple sentences, increased text load, and less repetition of high-frequency words.

Level 3 advances early-fluent readers toward fluency through increased text and concept load, less reliance on visuals, longer sentences, and more literary language.

Level 4 builds reading stamina by providing more text per page, increased use of punctuation, greater variation in sentence patterns, and increasingly challenging vocabulary.

Level 5 encourages children to move from "learning to read" to "reading to learn" by providing even more text, varied writing styles, and less familiar topics.

Whichever book is right for your reader, Blastoff! Readers are the perfect books to build confidence and encourage a love of reading that will last a lifetime!

This edition first published in 2019 by Bellwether Media, Inc.

No part of this publication may be reproduced in whole or in part without written permission of the publisher. For information regarding permission, write to Bellwether Media, Inc., Attention: Permissions Department, 6012 Blue Circle Drive, Minnetonka, MN 55343.

Library of Congress Cataloging-in-Publication Data

Names: Bowman, Chris, 1990- author.
Title: Skyscrapers / by Chris Bowman.
Description: Minneapolis, MN : Bellwether Media, Inc., 2019. | Series:
   Blastoff! Readers. Everyday Engineering | Includes bibliographical
   references and index. | Audience: Ages 5-8. | Audience: Grades K to 3.
Identifiers: LCCN 2018000221 (print) | LCCN 2018001457 (ebook) | ISBN
   9781626178250 (hardcover : alk. paper) | ISBN 9781681035666 (ebook)
Subjects: LCSH: Skyscrapers–Juvenile literature.
Classification: LCC TH1615 (ebook) | LCC TH1615 .B69 2019 (print) | DDC 720/.483–dc23
LC record available at https://lccn.loc.gov/2018000221

Editor: Paige V. Polinsky   Designer: Jeffrey Kollock

Printed in the United States of America, North Mankato, MN

Table of **Contents**

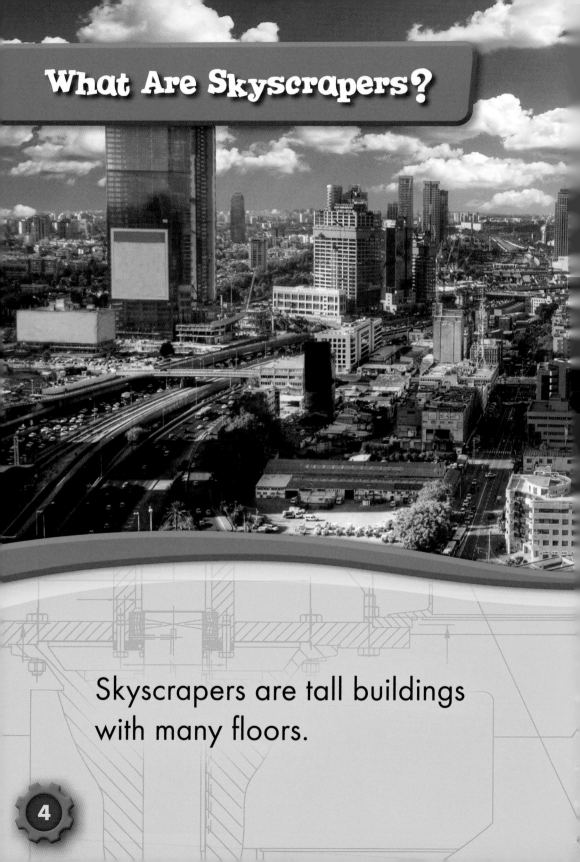

What Are Skyscrapers?

Skyscrapers are tall buildings with many floors.

They save space in big cities.
People can live, work, and
shop in skyscrapers.

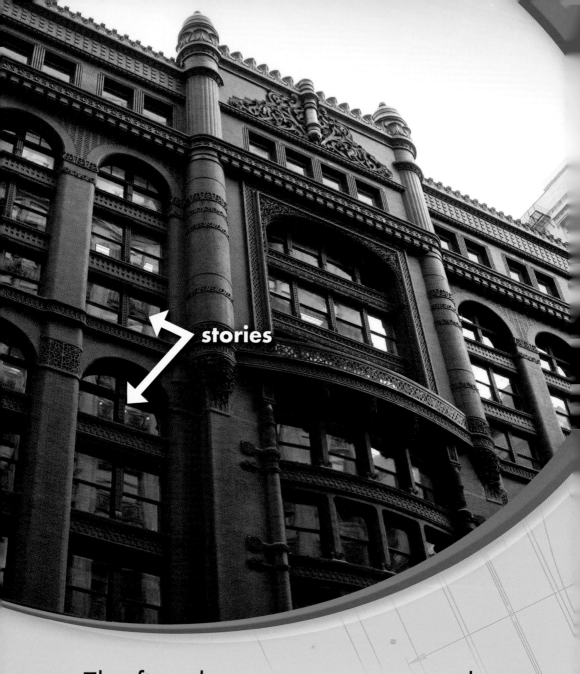

stories

The first skyscrapers were used for businesses. They were only about 10 **stories** tall.

These buildings were made of brick and iron. Steel helped later skyscrapers rise taller.

steel

Today, skyscrapers are much taller. **Elevators** carry people from floor to floor.

elevators

The buildings are made
of steel and **concrete**.
This makes them extra strong.

Types of Skyscrapers

Skyscrapers come in many looks. Most have a tube shape. These look like tall boxes.

Some are made of several tubes reaching different heights. These are bundled tubes.

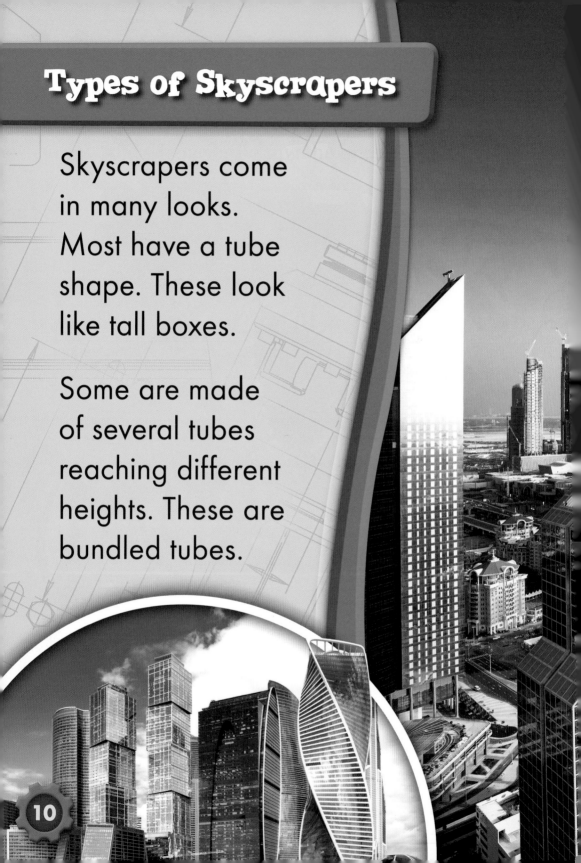

Famous Structure Profile
Burj Khalifa

Location: Dubai, United Arab Emirates

Type: bundled tube skyscraper

Year Completed: 2010

Architect: Adrian Smith; Skidmore, Owings, and Merrill LLP

Height: 2,717 feet (828 meters)

Stories: 162

11

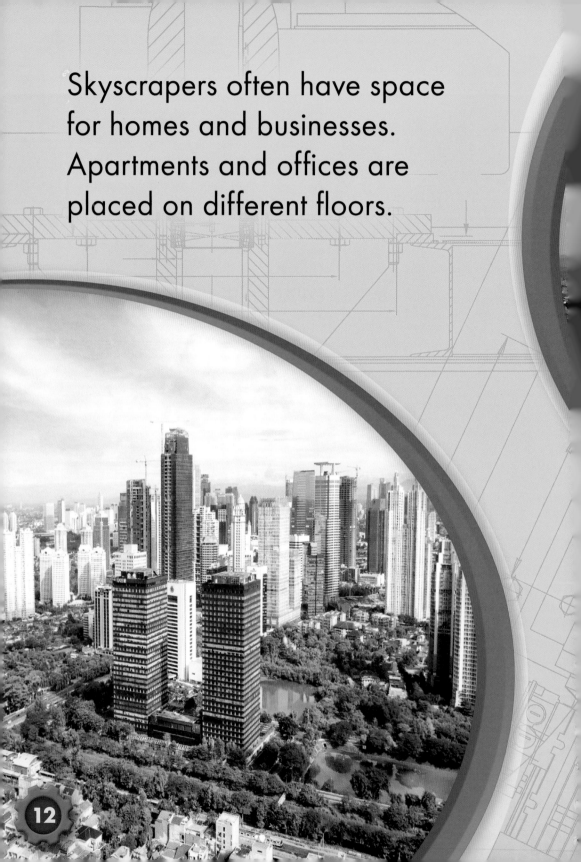

Skyscrapers often have space for homes and businesses. Apartments and offices are placed on different floors.

observation deck

Many skyscrapers have **observation decks** at the top for city views.

How Do Skyscrapers Work?

Most skyscrapers are built on **bedrock**. Their concrete bases are buried under the ground.

These wide bases hold
the **load** of the buildings.

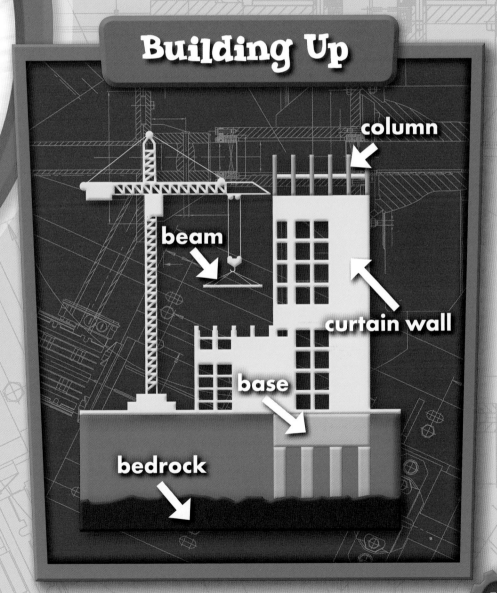

Building Up

column

beam

curtain wall

base

bedrock

columns

A grid of **columns** and beams
makes a skyscraper's frame.
These are often concrete and steel.

Glass **curtain walls** let light in.

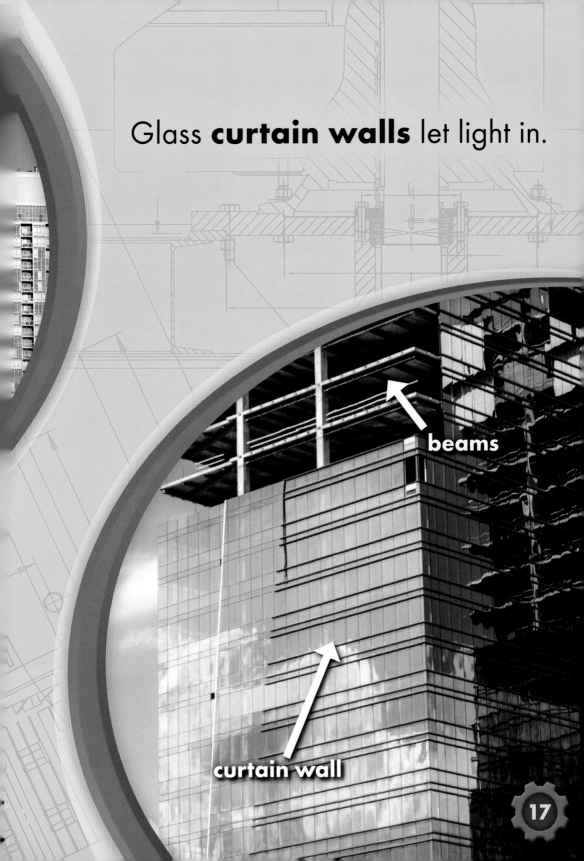

beams

curtain wall

Dampers at Work

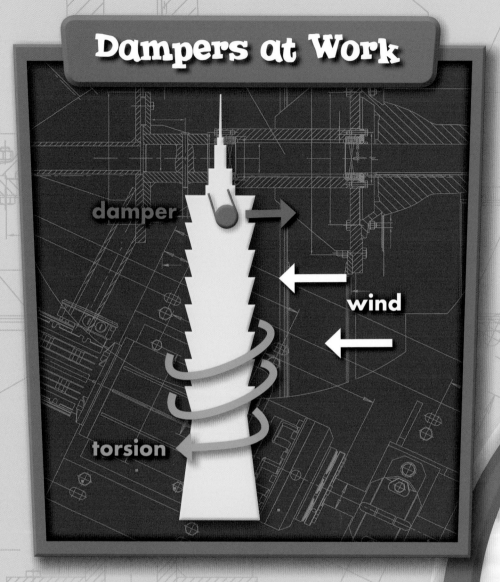

damper

wind

torsion

Skyscrapers must stay up in **earthquakes** and heavy winds. These cause **torsion** on buildings.

Dampers and strong frames keep skyscrapers steady.

damper

New skyscrapers are being built in creative shapes. They look like art.

They are also growing taller and taller. The sky is the limit!

Glossary

bedrock—a hard layer of stone under the ground on which buildings are built

columns—upright beams

concrete—a hard building material made of stone, cement, and water

curtain walls—large windows on skyscrapers

dampers—parts of skyscrapers that keep them steady in wind and earthquakes; dampers are heavy objects near the top of buildings.

earthquakes—sudden shaking movements in the ground

elevators—platforms inside skyscrapers that raise and lower people

load—weight or pressure

observation decks—floors or platforms for sightseeing

stories—floors in a building

torsion—a twisting force that acts on skyscrapers

To Learn More

AT THE LIBRARY
Marsico, Katie. *Skyscrapers*. New York, N.Y.:
Children's Press, 2016.

Polinsky, Paige V. *Skyscrapers*. Minneapolis, Minn.:
Abdo Pub., 2017.

Romero, Libby. *National Geographic Skyscrapers*.
Washington, D.C.: National Geographic, 2017.

ON THE WEB
Learning more about
skyscrapers is as
easy as 1, 2, 3.

1. Go to www.factsurfer.com.

2. Enter "skyscrapers" into the search box.

3. Click the "Surf" button and you will see a
   list of related web sites.

With factsurfer.com, finding more information is
just a click away.

Index